FIRST
LOOK AT

MOUNTAINS

For a free color catalog describing Gareth Stevens' list of high-quality children's books, call 1-800-341-3569 (USA) or 1-800-461-9120 (Canada).

Library of Congress Cataloging-in-Publication Data

Baker, Susan, 1961-
    First look at mountains / Susan Baker.
       p. cm. — (First look)
    "North American edition"—T.p. verso.
    Includes bibliographical references and index.
    Summary: Examines the formation, weather conditions, animal life, and recreational
possibilities of mountains.
    ISBN 0-8368-0703-0
    1. Mountains—Juvenile literature. [1. Mountains.] I. Title. II. Series.
GB512.B354 1991
551.4'32—dc20   91-9420

North American edition first published in 1991 by

Gareth Stevens Children's Books
1555 North RiverCenter Drive, Suite 201
Milwaukee, Wisconsin 53212, USA

U.S. edition copyright © 1991 by Gareth Stevens, Inc. First published as *Mountains*
in the United Kingdom, copyright © 1991, by Simon & Schuster Young Books.
Additional end matter copyright © 1991 by Gareth Stevens, Inc.

Photograph credits: John Cleare, 17, 18, 21; Department of the Environment (UK), 19; ZEFA, all others

Series editor: Patricia Lantier-Sampon
Design: M&M Design Partnership
Cover design: Laurie Shock
Layout: Sharone Burris

Printed in the United States of America

1 2 3 4 5 6 7 8 9 97 96 95 94 93 92 91

FIRST
LOOK AT

SUSAN BAKER

MOUNTAINS

Gareth Stevens Children's Books

MILWAUKEE

CONTENTS

6

MOUNTAIN VIEWS

Mountains are huge masses of rock that rise up from valleys and plains. Have you ever seen a mountain?

Climbing a steep mountain is hard work, but it can be fun. Just wait until you see the view!

THE LAST WILDERNESS

The rugged mountain wilderness is a difficult place for people to reach. Wild plants, birds, and other animals can live there undisturbed.

What wildlife would you look for if you were in the mountains?

9

10

MOUNTAIN PEOPLE

People live in some mountain areas. Why do you think the farmers who live there keep animals?

Sometimes the fields in these areas look like wide steps cut into the steep slopes. These steps are called terraces.

MINES AND QUARRIES

Sometimes there is a huge gash in a mountainside where people dig out stone. What do you think this stone is used for?

Can you think of anything else that is mined or quarried from mountains?

13

HOW WERE MOUNTAINS MADE?

Earth's restless crust has slowly shifted and crumpled, pushing up huge folds of rock to form mountains.

Rain, wind, and water wear rock away. Huge rocks turn into sandy grains that end up in the soil or at the bottom of the sea.

15

SNOW, ICE, AND GLACIERS

It can be very, very cold at the top of the highest mountains.

Snow falls instead of rain. Water turns to rivers of ice. Freezing frost makes the rocks crack and crumble.

WIND AND WEATHER

You must be equipped for all types of
weather when you go into the mountains.
The weather can change suddenly.

Would you enjoy the challenge and
adventure of exploring these wild,
lonely places?

MOUNTAINEERING

People who go on mountaineering expeditions have to carry everything with them that they need to survive.

Can you think of ten things they should take? How do you think they get water?

ROCK CLIMBING

Some mountains have long, gentle slopes.
Others are steep and rocky. Some climbers
choose the hard way to the top!

Rock climbing can be difficult and dangerous.
Special equipment and proper training are
important for climbs like these.

23

SNOW SPORTS

People all around the world enjoy the mountains in summer and winter. Sometimes they use special trains, cable cars, or lifts for the uphill journey.

Skiers swish downhill over the snow. Have you ever been in the snow? What snow sport do you like best?

25

MOUNTAIN RAILWAYS

Some people like to walk to the top of a mountain. Others like to take the train to admire the view.

Mountain railways have special tracks and engines for climbing steep slopes.

MOUNTAIN BARRIERS

Long, winding roads and railways have been built over mountain ranges. Tunnels have been cut through some mountains.

Sometimes people fly over mountains. How would you like to cross them?

29

More Books about Mountains

Animals in the Mountains. Raintree Publishers Staff (Raintree)
Climbing a Mountain with Mr. and Mrs. Bumba. Harwood (Lerner Publications)
Glaciers. Georges (Childrens Press)
I Love to Ski. Hulbert (Windswept House)
Mountain Wildlife. Dunmire (Pegasus Graphics)
The Mountains. Rius and Parramon (Barron's Educational Series)
Mountains. Stone (Childrens Press)
Mountains and Volcanoes. Curran (Troll Associates)
Rock Climbing. (Capstone Press)
Skiing: Speedy Slopes and Fluffy Snow in Ski School. Smith and Pelkowski (Barron's Educational Series)
Skiing Is for Me. Chappell (Lerner Publications)
The Surprise in the Mountains. Carlson (Harper & Row Junior Books)
What Is a Mountain? Arvetis (Macmillan)
When I Was Young in the Mountains. Rylant (Dutton)

Glossary

Cable car: A car that runs on special tracks like a train and is set up to be pulled along by strong ropes, or cables. A cable car can also hang from a cable that is set up along a roadway or up above the landscape. Many people use cable cars to get to the tops of mountains or other high places.

Crust: The outer part of the Earth's surface. The Earth's crust moves around and sometimes folds to produce mountains.

Glacier: A huge layer of ice that runs through valleys or across other large land areas.

Lift: A special machine that works much like an elevator and that is used to raise things or people to higher levels. People who ski often use ski lifts to take them to the tops of mountains.

Mine: A place under the ground that is rich with minerals. People called miners dig in the ground to take these minerals out.

Mountaineering: The sport of climbing mountains. Mountaineering can be very exciting, but it can also be dangerous.

Plain: A large area of flat land.

Quarry: A large pit or open space in the ground that has been dug up by people. Quarries usually have big deposits of certain types of stone or rock.

Steep: Having a sharp slope. Some mountains are very steep and dangerous.

Tunnel: A passageway built under the ground to help people get from one place to another. Going through a tunnel is sometimes the best way to get to the other side of a mountain.

Valley: A piece of lowland that lies between hills or mountains. The tops of some high mountains were once part of valley floors that were pushed up as layers of the Earth folded.

Wilderness: An area of land that has not been cultivated or settled by people.

Index

A number that is in **boldface** type means that the page has a picture of the subject on it.